HIGH Bush
TIDE Theatre

RUST

by Kenny Emson

Rust premiered at the Bush Theatre, London, on 26 June 2019, before transferring to the Edinburgh Festival Fringe and HighTide Festival Aldeburgh 2019.

RUST

CAST

NADIA   Claire Lams
DANIEL   Jon Foster

CREATIVE TEAM

Writer   Kenny Emson
Director   Eleanor Rhode
Designer   Max Johns
Lighting Designer   Jess Bernberg
Sound Designer   David Gregory
Lighting Associate   Kieron Johnson
Associate Director   Natalie Denton
Casting Director   Sophie Parrott CDG
Production Manager   Marco Savo
Stage Manager   Julia Nimmo

CAST

JON FOSTER | DANIEL

Theatre includes: *Dear Elizabeth, The Unknown Island, Idomeneus, Trojan Women, Dream Story, Mud* (Gate); *Every Day I Make Greatness Happen* (Hampstead); *Othello* (Shakespeare's Globe); *F*ck The Polar Bears* (Bush); *Buckets* (Orange Tree); *All I Want* (UK tour); *Cheese* (fanSHEN); *A Beginning A Middle and an End, Tenet* (Greyscale); *Invisible* (Transport); *The Alchemist* (Firehouse Creative); *A New Way To Please You, His Fall, Speaking Like Magpies, Thomas More* (RSC); *How To Tell the Monsters from the Misfits* (Birmingham REP); *Long Time Dead* (Paines Plough); *After Haggerty* (Finborough); *Food* (Traverse); *Dr Jekyll and Mr Hyde* (Babayaga Theatre Company); *Free from Sorrow* (Living Pictures); *Romeo and Juliet* (Creation Theatre Company); *Oliver Twist* (Instant Classics); *The Melancholy Hussar* (Etcetera); *Two Gentlemen of Verona* (Pentameters); *Treasure Island* (Palace); *The Bear* (The Bear).

Television includes: *Sanditon* (Red Planet Ltd); *Prime Suspect 1973* (Noho for ITC); *Fortitude* (Tiger Aspect); *Da Vinci's Demons* (BBC Worldwide/Starz); *The Great Fire* (Ecosse Films); *New Tricks* (Wall to Wall Television for the BBC); *Rev* (Big Talk Productions); *Mrs Biggs, Come Rain Come Shine* (ITV); *Abroad* (Abroad Films); *Eastenders, Silent Witness, The Last Enemy* (BBC); *Law and Order* (Kudos); *The Bill* (Thames Television); *Clone* (Roughcut); *The IT Crowd* (Talkback); *Instinct* (Granada).

Film includes: *The Rabbi and The Tooth* (Zoe Griesdale-Sherry Productions); *Alba* (Rabblewise Films); *Tides* (Elation Pictures); *Nice Guy* (Red Bike Films); *Love's Kitchen* (Eyeline Entertainment).

Radio includes: *The Duchess of Malfi* (BBC World Service).

CLAIRE LAMS | NADIA

Theatre includes: *Paradise* (Hampstead); *Kiss Me* (Hampstead/Trafalgar Studios); *The Lottery of Love* (Orange Tree); *The King's Speech* (Chichester/Birmingham Rep); *The Little Mermaid* (Bristol Old Vic); *Routes, Harvest* (Royal Court); *One Man, Two Guvnors* (Broadway/West End/National Theatre); *The Spies in Room 502* (Latitude Festival); *W11* (Gate); *While You Lie* (Traverse); *Educating Rita* (Watermill); *Absent Friends* (Watford Palace Theatre); *The Miracle, DNA, Baby Girl* (National Theatre); *Faustus* (Headlong); *Fabulation* (Tricycle); *Presence* (Theatre Royal Plymouth); *Chimps* (Liverpool Everyman); *Citizenship* (National Theatre Studio); *Fields of Gold, Soap* (Stephen Joseph Theatre); *Coming Around Again, Huddersfield* (West Yorkshire Playhouse); *The Happiest Days of Your Life* (Royal Exchange Theatre, Manchester); *The Dice House* (Birmingham Stage Company).

Television includes: *Casualty, Call the Midwife, The Wrong Mans, Silent Witness, Doctors, Holby City, EastEnders* (BBC); *Humans* (Kudos); *Obsessed* (October Films); *Random* (Hillbilly Television); *The Bill* (Thames Television); *The Brief* (Granada Television).

Film includes: *Beyond the Blade* (The Guardian); *Pumpkin Head 4* (Clubdeal PH Film Company); *Southwalk The Movie* (T-Max Media); *Danielle* (Independent Film).

CREATIVES

KENNY EMSON | WRITER

Kenny is an award-winning playwright and screenwriter.

His plays include *Quadrophenia* (Mercury); *Parkway Dreams* (Sir John Mills Theatre); *Terrorism* (Bush); *This Must be the Place* (Vault Festival – co-written with Brad Birch) and *Plastic* (Old Red Lion). He was co-creator, co-writer and associate producer on the BAFTA Craft, SXSW and Prix Italia nominated *The Last Hours of Laura K* and adapted Agatha Christie's *The Coming of Mister Quin* which was nominated for a BAFTA CYMRU games award. He has written for *EastEnders*, *Doctors*, BBC Radio 3 and 4 and has been shortlisted for the Bruntwood, Red Planet and Papatango Prizes as well as winning the Adrienne Benham, Off West End Adopt a Playwright and Mercury/Weinberger Playwriting Awards.

ELEANOR RHODE | DIRECTOR

Eleanor is an Associate Artist for HighTide, for whom she directed the musical *Thor and Loki* for the Edinburgh and HighTide Festivals with Vicky Graham Productions. Her most recent work includes the world premiere of *Boudica* by Tristan Bernays for the Globe Theatre; *Blue Door* for Theatre Royal Bath; and *Wendy and Peter Pan* for The Royal Lyceum in Edinburgh.

In 2009 she co-founded Snapdragon Productions to bring neglected and unknown works to new audiences. Work for Snapdragon includes the critically acclaimed production of *Toast* by Richard Bean (UK tour/New York), which was nominated for Best Touring Production at the 2016 UK Theatre Awards; and the award-winning world premiere of musical *Teddy* by Tristan Bernays and Dougal Irvine, which she revived last year for a national tour and London run at the Vaults.

Other recent work includes: *Frankenstein* (Watermill/Wilton's Music Hall); *Terrorism* (Bush); *Beauty and the Beast* (Watford Palace Theatre); *When We Were Women* (Orange Tree); *Toast*, *Thark* (Park); *Generous*, *The Drawer Boy*, *A Life* (Finborough) and the world premiere of the musical *For All That* for Centerstage Theater, Seattle.

Forthcoming productions include *King John* for the Royal Shakespeare Company.

MAX JOHNS | DESIGNER

Max trained in theatre design at Bristol Old Vic Theatre School and was the recipient of a BBC Performing Arts Fellowship in 2015. Prior to this he worked for a number of years as a designer in Germany. His most recent UK productions include *Strange Fruit* (Bush); *The Half God of Rainfall* (Kiln/Birmingham Rep/Fuel); *Wendy and Peter Pan* (Royal Lyceum Edinburgh); *Kes*, *Random* (Leeds Playhouse); *Utility*, *Twelfth Night* (Orange Tree); *Buggy Baby* (The Yard); *Yellowman* (Young Vic); *Baddies* (Synergy Theatre Project); *Fidelo* (London Philharmonic Orchestra); *Enron* (Theatre Royal Bath); *There Shall Be Fireworks* (Plasticine Men); *Life Raft*, *Medusa*, *Under A Cardboard Sea* (Bristol Old Vic); *Strawberry And Chocolate* (Tobacco Factory Theatres); *Infinity Pool* (Bedlam); *Bucket List* (Theatre Ad Infinitum); *Hamlet*, *All's Well That Ends Well* (Shakespeare at the Tobacco Factory). Max has also had work produced at the V&A and Theatre Royal Bath. Forthcoming productions include *King John* at the Royal Shakespeare Company, directed by Eleanor Rhode.

JESS BERNBERG I LIGHTING DESIGNER

Jess is a London based Lighting Designer. She trained at Guildhall School of Music and Drama and was the 2018 Laboratory Associate Lighting Designer at Nuffield Southampton Theatres. Her designs include: *Songlines* (HighTide); *Rejoicing At Her Wondrous Vulva The Young Woman Applauded Herself* (Ovalhouse); *Out of Water, Cougar* (Orange Tree); *The Crucible, Sex Sex Men Men, A New and Better You, Buggy Baby* (The Yard); *The Town That Trees Built* (Young Vic); *And the Rest of Me Floats* (Birmingham Rep/Bush); *The Borrowers* (Tobacco Factory); *Fabric, Drip Feed* (Soho); *Victoria's Knickers, Consensual* (NYT); *Medusa, Much Ado About Nothing, Dungeness, Love and Information* (Nuffield Southampton Theatres); *Homos, or Everyone in America* (Finborough); *Punk Rock, Pomona* (New Diorama/Mountview); *Devil with the Blue Dress, FCUK'D* (Off West End Award nomination) (The Bunker).

In 2017 Jess was awarded the Association of Lighting Designers' Francis Reid Award.

DAVID GREGORY I SOUND DESIGNER

David has sound designed many productions across the West End, UK and internationally. He won the TTA Award for Sound in 2015. He is an associate sound designer at The Watermill Theatre in Newbury. David's most recent and upcoming credits include: *King John* (RSC); *A Midsummer Night's Dream* and *Macbeth* (Watermill/UK tour); *Pope* (Royal & Derngate); *Blue Door* (Theatre Royal Bath); *Cat In The Hat* (Curve/UK tour); *Fantasia* (Vaults); *Thor & Loki* (Assembly Roxy); *Tartuffe* (Theatre Royal Haymarket); *Twelfth Night* (Wilton's Music Hall); *The Selfish Giant* (Vaudeville/Northampton); *A Midsummer Night's Dream* (Watermill); *George's Marvellous Medicine* (Curve/UK tour); *The Borrowers* (Watermill); *Boudica* (Shakespeare's Globe); *Bombay Roxy* (Dishoom); *Cunning Vixen* (ENO/Silent Opera); *Gabriel* (UK tour); *Twelfth Night* and *Romeo and Juliet* (Watermill/Euro tour); *Grapes of Wrath* (UK tour/Nuffield); *Frankenstein* (Wilton's Music Hall); *These Trees are Made of Blood* (Arcola); *Terrorism* (Bush); *Queens of Syria* (Young Vic/UK tour); *Alice in Wonderland* (Watermill); *The First Man* (Jermyn Street Theatre); *Our Friend The Enemy* (UK/NYC); *Pocket Merchant* (Propeller Theatre Company); *When We Were Woman* (Orange Tree).

KIERON JOHNSON I LIGHTING ASSOCIATE

Kieron is a Lighting Designer based in Leeds and works in Theatre and Contemporary Dance.

Previous credits include: *the sea tells a story* (Ben Wright); *99 Moves* and *Vanishing Points* (Zoi Dimitriou); *FIM* (Theo 'TJ' Lowe); *Tides* (Joss Arnott); *Nothing & Being, Being & Nothing* (Gary Lambert); *At The End We Begin* (Richard Chappell); *Misura* (Hubert Essakow); *Aperture* (Kerry Nicholls); *(Im)Pulse* (Dam Van Huynh); *Everything Between Us, You're Human Like The Rest Of Them* (Finborough); *Thirst* (The Space); *Wasted* (King's Head); *Songlines* (HighTide/Associate LD); *Run* (JW3/Bunker/Associate LD).

NATALIE DENTON I ASSOCIATE DIRECTOR

Natalie Denton was one of the Jerwood Assistant Directors at the Young Vic in 2017, assisting Benedict Andrews on *Cat on a Hot Tin Roof* at the Apollo Theatre, starring Sienna Miller and Jack O'Connell. More recently, she has worked as assistant director with Headlong Theatre and Mark Rubenstein Ltd. on developing *Richard III* and *Sing Street* respectively. She is currently exploring film production with a view to working in television and film development in the future and was on a placement at Revolution Films Ltd.

Other theatre credits include: As Director: *Breathe* (Bread & Roses); *Five Plays: Nuclear* (Young Vic); *RWR: The Birthday Party* (Theatre503); *Fingertips* (Edinburgh Fringe Festival); *At First Sight* (Karamel Club).

As Assistant Director: *Teddy* (UK tour/Southwark Playhouse); *Years of Sunlight* (Theatre503); *13* (Unicorn).

SOPHIE PARROTT CDG I CASTING DIRECTOR

Theatre credits include: *Songlines* (HighTide); *Sweeney Todd, Othello, Paint Your Wagon, Clockwork Orange, The Big I Am, A Midsummer Night's Dream* (Liverpool Everyman); *One Night In Miami, Wonderland* (remount); *Shebeen* (Nottingham Playhouse); *An Octoroon* (Orange Tree/National Theatre); *Blood Knot, The March On Russia* (Orange Tree); *The Crucible, Buggy Baby, This Beautiful Future* (The Yard); *Big Aftermath of a Small Disclosure, Winter Solstice* (Actors Touring Company); *The Claim* (Shoreditch Town Hall/national tour); *All The President's Men?, Pomona* (additional casting; National Theatre); *Death of a Salesman* (Royal & Derngate/ tour); *Wish List, Yen* (Royal Court/Royal Exchange Theatre, Manchester); *A Streetcar Named Desire* (co-casting director, Royal Exchange Theatre, Manchester); *Bird* (Sherman Cymru/Royal Exchange Theatre, Manchester); *Britannia Waves the Rules* (tour); *Billy Liar* (Royal Exchange Theatre, Manchester); *My Mother Said I Never Should* (St James); *The Crocodile* (Manchester International Festival).

Casting Director TV credits include: *Call the Midwife* (Series 9); *Doctors* (BBC).

Casting Associate and Assistant TV credits include: *Howards End, Delicious* (two series); *Rillington Place, Thirteen, Call the Midwife* (five series); *Silent Witness* (two series); *The Game, Esio Trot, Mr Stink, WPC56, The Preston Passion, The Night Watch, Holby City* (four series); *The Riots: In Their Own Words, Undeniable*.

Film credits include: *The Secret Agent, Whirlpool, A Street Cat Named Bob* (as Casting Associate).

Sophie was recently nominated for 'Best Casting in a Theatre Production' at the Casting Directors' Guild Awards for *An Octoroon* (Orange Tree/National Theatre).

MARCO SAVO I PRODUCTION MANAGER

Marco is a Production Manager and New Media Art Curator currently working with eStage as a Production Manager for theatres in London and the UK. He is restless, passionate and creatively committed, and considers art as the most powerful form of communication. His entire career has been devoted to support artistic expression and deliver it to communities.

He has been running a wide range of events for over six years in theatres, art galleries, clubs and cultural venues across Barcelona and London.

Marco is the founder of Audiovisual City (www.audiovisualcity.org) a worldwide magazine of Audiovisual Culture. Nowadays it is the most important online magazine of AV artists and events.

JULIA NIMMO I STAGE MANAGER

Julia trained in Design for Theatre and Television at Charles Stuart University, Wagga Wagga, Australia. As a Stage Manager her theatre credits include: *The Trick* (HighTide/Bush/UK tour); *Songlines* (HighTide/Edinburgh Fringe Festival 2018 and 2018 UK tour); *Harrogate* (HighTide/Royal Court/UK tour); *Lampedusa* (HighTide/Soho); *Macbeth* (Wildfire Productions/Cell Block Theatre, Sydney); *The Beauty Queen of Leenane* (Wildfire Productions, Seymour Centre, Sydney); *The Real Thing* (English Touring Theatre, 2012 UK tour); *The One* (Soho); *Beached* (Marlowe/Soho); *Flare Path* (Birdsong Productions/Original Theatre, 2016 UK tour); *This Much* (Moving Dust/Soho Theatre); *Edward II* (The Marlowe Society/Cambridge Arts Theatre); *All the Things I Lied About* (Paul Jellis Ltd/Soho/2017 UK tour); *Frankie Vah* (Paul Jellis Ltd, Soho/2018 UK tour); *Paper, Scissors, Stone* (Tara Finney Productions/The Vaults Festival 2018/Live Theatre); *Witches* (Hertfordshire County Youth Theatre, Watford Palace). Festival credits include: *WOW Festival* (Hull 2017); *Talawa Firsts Festival* (2017 and 2018).

Julia was awarded 'Best Individual Stage Manager' at the SMA National Stage Management Awards 2019.

H|GH
T|DE

NEW THEATRE FOR
ADVENTUROUS PEOPLE

HighTide is a theatre company and charity based in East Anglia that has an unparalleled twelve-year history of successfully launching the careers of emerging British playwrights.

Our alumni speak for themselves: Luke Barnes, Adam Brace, Tallulah Brown, E V Crowe, Elinor Cook, Rob Drummond, Thomas Eccleshare, Theresa Ikoko, Branden Jacobs-Jenkins, Eve Leigh, Anders Lustgarten, Joel Horwood, Ella Hickson, Harry Melling, Nessah Muthy, Vinay Patel, Nick Payne, Phil Porter, Beth Steel, Al Smith, Sam Steiner, Molly Taylor, Jack Thorne and Frances Ya-Chu Cowhig.

We have staged productions with the highest quality theatres across the UK, from the Traverse in Edinburgh, to the Royal Exchange in Manchester, Theatre Royal Bath and the National Theatre in London. We discover new talent, provide creative development opportunities for playwrights and other creatives, and stage high quality theatre productions both in our region and nationally through our festivals and touring.

We enable new and underrepresented playwrights to express their visions of contemporary politics and society, demonstrate their creative potential and therein showcase the future of theatre.

BackstageTrust

HIGH TIDE

2019

TWELVE YEARS OF SHAPING THE MAINSTREAM

Our twelfth season under Artistic Director Steven Atkinson, began in February 2019 with Eve Leigh's **The Trick**, directed by Roy Alexander Weise in a HighTide and Loose Tongue co-production. **The Trick** premiered at the Bush Theatre before embarking on an national tour.

In April, **Mouthpiece** by Kieran Hurley, presented by Traverse Theatre in association with HighTide transferred to Soho Theatre after a successful run at Traverse Theatre in December 2018. It will return to Edinburgh in August as part of the Traverse's Edinburgh Festival Fringe 2019 season.

Rust by Kenny Emson, directed by Eleanor Rhode, will be presented in a HighTide and Bush Theatre co-production in June 2019 at the Bush Theatre. **Rust** will transfer to the Edinburgh Festival Fringe before running at HighTide Festival in September 2019.

HighTide, in partnership with Assembly Roxy, launch **Disruption: The Future of New Theatre** as part of the Edinburgh Festival Fringe 2019. **Disruption** will present a curated programme of provocative and contemporary new theatre. Alongside **Rust**, HighTide will co-produce a further four productions: **Pops** by Charlotte Josephine, **Collapsible** by Margaret Perry, **Since U Been Gone** by Teddy Lamb & **Pink Lemonade** by Mia Johnson.

Former HighTide First Commissions Writer Sophie Ellerby will premiere **LIT** in September 2019, directed by Stef O'Driscoll in a HighTide and Nottingham Playhouse co-production. **LIT** will debut at the HighTide Festival before transferring to Nottingham Playhouse.

Finally, HighTide are partnering with **BBC Radio 3** and **BBC Arts** on two new radio plays by HighTide alumni writers Tallulah Brown and Vinay Patel. These plays will be presented at HighTide Festival in 2019 with a live recording to be broadcast later this year.

For full details, visit hightide.org.uk

HIGH TIDE

HIGHTIDE THEATRE

24a St John Street, London, EC1M 4AY
0207 566 9765 - hello@hightide.org.uk - hightide.org.uk

H|GH T|DE

BE A FRIEND OF THE FESTIVAL

"There are very talented young playwrights in the UK and if they are lucky they will find their way to HighTide Theatre. I hope you will join me in supporting this remarkable and modest organisation. With your help HighTide can play an even more major role in the promoting of new writing in the UK."
Lady Susie Sainsbury, Backstage Trust

Our Friends are an important part of HighTide. Our benefits include:
- An invite to the Festival programme launch party in Aldeburgh
- An invite to the Artists and Friends Brunch during the Festival
- Dedicated ticket booking service and access to house seats for sold out events

From as little as £10 a month, your contribution will support the Festival in providing:
- Performance tickets to local school children
- Workshops on performance and writing
- The Summer Connect club in Aldeburgh for the next generation of playwrights

All of which we can provide at no cost to local young people, thanks to the generosity of our Friends.

Be a Friend for as little as £10 per month, or become a Best Friend for as little as £25 per month.

To make a one-off contribution, please call our offices on 01728 687110 quoting `Friends of the Festival', or email **rowan@hightide.org.uk**.

We are thankful to all of our supporters, without whom our work simply would not take place.

HighTide Theatre is a National Portfolio Organisation of the Arts Council England

Bush Theatre

Bush Theatre, 7 Uxbridge Road, London W12 8LJ
Box Office: 020 8743 5050 | Administration: 020 8743 3584

Email: info@bushtheatre.co.uk
bushtheatre.co.uk

Alternative Theatre Company Ltd
(The Bush Theatre) is a Registered Charity and a company limited by guarantee.
Registered in England no. 1221968 Charity no. 270080

Bush
Theatre
We make theatre
for London. Now.

The Bush is a world-famous home for new plays
and an internationally renowned champion of
playwrights. We discover, nurture and produce
the best new writers from the widest range of
backgrounds from our home in a distinctive corner
of west London.

The Bush has won over 100 awards and developed
an enviable reputation for touring its acclaimed
productions nationally and internationally.

We are excited by exceptional new voices,
stories and perspectives – particularly those with
contemporary bite which reflect the vibrancy of
British culture now.

Located in the newly renovated old library on
Uxbridge Road in the heart of Shepherd's Bush,
the theatre houses two performance spaces, a
rehearsal room and the lively Library Bar.

bushtheatre.co.uk

THANK YOU

The Bush Theatre would like to thank all its supporters whose valuable contributions have helped us to create a platform for our future and to promote the highest quality new writing, develop the next generation of creative talent, lead innovative community engagement work and champion diversity.

LONE STAR
Gianni Alen-Buckley
Michael Alen-Buckley
Rafael & Anne-Helene Biosse Duplan
Alice Findlay
Charles Holloway
Miles Morland

HANDFUL OF STARS
Dawn & Gary Baker
Charlie Bigham
Judy Bollinger
Clive & Helena Butler
Grace Chan
Clare & Chris Clark
Clyde Cooper
Sue Fletcher
Richard & Jane Gordon
Priscilla John
Simon & Katherine Johnson
Philippa Seal & Philip Jones QC
Joanna Kennedy
V&F Lukey
Robert Ledger & Sally Mousdale
Georgia Oetker
Philip & Biddy Percival
Clare Rich
Joana & Henrik Schliemann
Lesley Hill & Russ Shaw
van Tulleken Family
and one anonymous donor.

RISING STARS
Nicholas Alt
Mark Bentley
David Brooks
Catharine Browne
Matthew Byam Shaw
Tim & Andrea Clark
Sarah Clarke
Claude & Susie Cochin de Billy
Lois Cox
Susie Cuff
Matthew Cushen
Philippa Dolphin
John Fraser
Jack Gordon & Kate Lacy
Hugh & Sarah Grootenhuis
Jessica Ground
Thea Guest
Patrick Harrison
Roberta Jaffe-Wilcockson
Ann & Ravi Joseph
Davina & Malcolm Judelson
Miggy Littlejohns
Isabella Macpherson

RISING STARS (continued)
Liz & Luke Mayhew
Michael McCoy
Judith Mellor
Caro Millington
Dan & Laurie Mucha
Mark & Anne Paterson
Barbara Prideaux
Emily Reeve
Renske & Marion
Saleem & Alexandra Siddiqi
Brian Smith
Peter Tausig
Guy Vincent & Sarah Mitchell
Trish Wadley
Amanda Waggott
and three anonymous donors.

SPONSORS & SUPPORTERS
AKA
Alen-Buckley LLP
Gianni & Michael Alen-Buckley
Jeremy Attard Manche
Bill & Judy Bollinger
Edward Bonham Carter
Martin Bowley
Duke & Duchess of Buccleuch
The Hon Mrs Louise Burness
Sir Charles & Lady Isabella Burrell
Philip & Tita Byrne
CHK Charities Limited
Peppe & Quentin Ciardi
Joanna & Hadyn Cunningham
Leo & Grega Daly
Patrick & Mairead Flaherty
Sue Fletcher
The Hon Sir Rocco Forte
The Hon Portia Forte
Mark Franklin
The Gatsby Charitable Foundation
The Right Hon Piers Gibson
Farid & Emilie Gragour
Victoria Gray
John Gordon
Vivienne Guinness
Melanie Hall
The Headley Trust
Brian Heyworth
Lesley Hill & Russ Shaw
Michael Holland & Denise O'Donoghue
Charles Holloway
Graham & Amanda Hutton
James Gorst Architects Ltd.
Simon & Katherine Johnson
Tarek & Diala Khlat

SPONSORS & SUPPORTERS (continued)
Bernard Lambilliotte
Marion Lloyd
The Lord Forte Foundation
Peter & Bettina Mallinson
Mahoro Charitable Trust
James Christopher Miller
Mitsui Fodosan (U.K.) Ltd
Alfred Munkenbeck III
Nick Hern Books
Georgia Oetker
RAB Capital
Kevin Pakenham
Sir Howard Panter
Joanna Prior
Josie Rourke
Lady Susie Sainsbury
Barry Serjent
Tim & Catherine Score
Search Foundation
Richard Sharp
Susie Simkins
Edward Snape & Marilyn Eardley
Michael & Sarah Spencer
Stanhope PLC
Ross Turner
The Syder Foundation
van Tulleken Family
Johnny & Dione Verulam
Robert & Felicity Waley-Cohen
Elizabeth Wigoder
Philip Wooller
Danny Wyler
and three anonymous donors.

TRUSTS AND FOUNDATIONS
The Andrew Lloyd Webber Foundation
The Boris Karloff Foundation
The Boshier-Hinton Foundation
The Bruce Wake Charitable Trust
The Chapman Charitable Trust
The City Bridge Trust
Cockayne—Grants for the Arts
The John S Cohen Foundation
The Daisy Trust
The Equity Charitable Trust
Esmée Fairbairn Foundation
Fidelio Charitable Trust
Foyle Foundation
Garfield Weston Foundation
Garrick Charitable Trust
Hammersmith United Charities
Heritage of London Trust
John Lyon's Charity
The J Paul Getty Jnr Charitable Trust

TRUSTS AND FOUNDATIONS (continued)
The John Thaw Foundation
The Kirsten Scott Memorial Trust
The Leverhulme Trust
The London Community Foundation
Margaret Guido's Charitable Trust
The Martin Bowley Charitable Trust
The Monument Trust
The Noel Coward Foundation
Paul Hamlyn Foundation
Peter Wolff Foundation
Pilgrim Trust
The Royal Victoria Hall Foundation
Sir John Cass's Foundation
Stavros Niarchos Foundation
The Theatres Trust
Viridor Credits
The Williams Charitable Trust
Western Riverside Environmental Fund
Worshipful Company of Mercers
The Wolfson Foundation
and one anonymous donor.

CORPORATE SPONSORS AND MEMBERS
The Agency (London) Ltd
Dorsett Shepherds Bush
Drama Centre London
Fever Tree
The Groucho Club
THE HOXTON
Philip Wooller
Westfield London

PUBLIC FUNDING

If you are interested in finding out how to be involved, please visit **bushtheatre.co.uk/support-us** or email **development@bushtheatre.co.uk** or call **020 8743 3584.**

RUST

Kenny Emson

Acknowledgements

Thanks to... Eleanor and Trevor. The incredible team at HighTide. All those at Bush past and present who helped get this back on. Sarah Liisa, Jodi, Matt and the rest of the gang at NHB. Emily and Georgie at The Agency. And, as ever, Ange... for putting up with me.

K.E.

For Sofie and Disco Di

Characters

DANIEL
NADIA

Author's Note

Throughout the play various items will be brought into the
room, things spilt, glass broken, bloodstains left. These
shouldn't be cleared until noted. The growing detritus and litter
should be a feature of the set, no matter how this affects the
actors' movement. An empty Ikea showroom to Tracey Emin's
bed isn't a million miles off. Or ignore me completely and do
something crazy. Just don't be boring. A rule to live by.

K.E.

*This text went to press before the end of rehearsals and so may
differ slightly from the play as performed.*

1.

(*The Flat.*

NADIA, *late thirties, stands in an empty living room. There is one door that leads off to a small kitchen and bathroom. The walls are whitewashed. The floor is that shiny fake-wood lining.*

There are no personal effects. No furniture. Just a bare mattress.

The sound of a toilet flushing from off. DANIEL, *late thirties, enters.*)

DANIEL   Mr and Mrs Smith?

(*Beat.*)

NADIA   You are <u>so</u> original.

DANIEL   Mr and Mrs Original?

NADIA   Do you want to get arrested?

DANIEL   I'm not sure they chuck people in prison for –

NADIA   It's forgery.

DANIEL   It's a name on a tenancy agreement.

NADIA   Which is a legally binding contract.

DANIEL   Fuck it's sexy when you talk down to me.

NADIA   Why draw more attention to ourselves?

DANIEL   We're a couple of boring, white, married, thirty-somethings –

NADIA   Oi!

DANIEL   The police are not going to break down the door and cart us off.

(*Beat.*)

Why don't we just use our own names?

NADIA   Bills.

DANIEL   Evidence.

NADIA   Exactly.

DANIEL   You've thought this through.

NADIA   I have.

DANIEL   I'm flattered.

(*Beat.*)

So your friend…

NADIA   My friend will help us out.

DANIEL   Isn't that nice of her.

NADIA   She has her sympathies.

DANIEL   She's a sympathiser. I wish I had friends like that.

NADIA   Then we should work on your personality.

DANIEL   You're in a funny mood.

NADIA   Mischievous. Not funny.

DANIEL   Maybe we could…

(*He makes a gesture.*)

NADIA   What was *that*?

DANIEL   You know.

(*She laughs knowingly.*)

NADIA   Now?

DANIEL   He said he won't be back for ten minutes.

NADIA   We still need to pick a name for the lease.

DANIEL   I can be quick.

NADIA   Just what every woman wants to hear.

DANIEL   Okay then, after. When we're done.

(*Beat.*)

NADIA   Where?

DANIEL   The Green.

NADIA   The Green!

DANIEL   Al fresco.

NADIA   It's a fucking roundabout.

DANIEL   A triangle, actually. A triangle-about.

NADIA   Not really the season. We need to wait until they *replant the shrubbery.*

DANIEL   There's going to be shrubbery?

NADIA   One can only hope.

(*Pause.*)

DANIEL   Your friend... Can we...

NADIA   I'm not into threesomes.

DANIEL   Can we trust her? No questions asked?

NADIA   A couple of questions. Answered.

DANIEL   But is she –

NADIA   You have to trust someone, Daniel.

DANIEL   I trust you.

NADIA   Good.

(*Beat.*)

Mr and Mrs White?

DANIEL   The Whites... They sound fun.

(*She steps towards him.*)

NADIA   They are.

(*Pause.*)

It is nice isn't it? You do like it.

DANIEL   I do.

NADIA   A home.

DANIEL   On Mondays.

NADIA   But still… A place. Our place.

DANIEL   *Our place*. That's sweet.

NADIA   I can be sweet.

DANIEL   Don't make a habit of it. I might get the wrong idea.

(*A moment. Then* NADIA *kisses him full on the mouth. The door starts to open. She moves away sharply.*)

2.

(NADIA *and* DANIEL *sit on the floor of the darkened room, curtains shut, with only some tealight candles illuminating the space.*

There are a couple of bottles of Prosecco next to them.)

NADIA   Weapons?

DANIEL   What kind?

NADIA   Use your imagination.

DANIEL   Whips?

NADIA   Knives.

DANIEL   Ouch.

NADIA   Yes or no?

DANIEL   No knives.

NADIA   But whips?

DANIEL   Yes.

NADIA   Good. Blindfolds?

DANIEL   Yes.

NADIA   Strangulation?

(*Pause.*)

DANIEL Yeah.

NADIA   You had to think about it.

DANIEL I'm a pussy.

NADIA   Belts?

DANIEL For what purpose?

NADIA   Every purpose.

DANIEL Yes.

NADIA   That's better. Don't overthink things. Ever.

DANIEL Where has thinking ever got anyone?

NADIA   Exactly.

DANIEL Go again.

NADIA   It's not my turn.

DANIEL Isn't it?

NADIA   No.

DANIEL Fuck I'm drunk.

NADIA   Lightweight.

DANIEL Some of us don't consider drinking a bottle of wine
        with lunch a life requirement.

NADIA   A job requirement.

DANIEL Whatever.

        (*Pause.*)

        I can't think of anything.

NADIA   You are a constant disappointment.

        (*Beat.*)

        Watersports?

DANIEL No.

NADIA   That was very definite.

DANIEL Not my thing.

NADIA Don't you like the idea of being dirty? Mucky?

DANIEL I don't think I could physically do it. I have to piss
sitting down when I go to the toilet in a pub.

NADIA Awwww.

DANIEL Thanks. That will help in future I'm sure.

NADIA It's okay. You haven't got anything to be worried
about. Down there.

DANIEL I've been waiting my whole life for someone to tell
me that.

NADIA Happy to oblige.

DANIEL It's a nerves thing. The pissing. Been like it since
I was a kid.

NADIA Were you a late developer?

DANIEL Have you ever had a shower with twenty other boys?

NADIA Yes.

DANIEL Filth.

NADIA You love it.

DANIEL Go again!

NADIA It's your turn!

DANIEL I can't think. All the blood has rushed out of my
brain to my massive –

NADIA Anal.

DANIEL Anal?

NADIA Yeah. Anal.

(*Pause.*)

DANIEL Yeah.

NADIA Giving and receiving?

DANIEL Fuck it. Why not. In for a penny… You?

NADIA   Yes.

DANIEL   You've tried it before?

NADIA   No.

DANIEL   It's just some girls...

NADIA   *Girls.*

DANIEL   Some girls –

NADIA   Do I seem like *some girls* to you?

DANIEL   No. No, you really don't.

(*He kisses her. Hard. Felt.*)

NADIA   Other people?

DANIEL   I thought you didn't do threesomes?

NADIA   I could be convinced.

DANIEL   Really?

NADIA   Maybe.

DANIEL   Have you got a girlfriend who –

NADIA   Why do men always assume a threesome needs two women?

DANIEL   Have you seen the male anatomy? It's like a cruel joke. Who needs two of them bouncing around in a bed?

NADIA   We don't have a bed.

DANIEL   How modern of us.

NADIA   I wouldn't want to share you.

DANIEL   You already do.

(*A silence.*)

NADIA   Well, that's a mood-killer.

DANIEL   I'm a fucking idiot.

NADIA   It's okay.

DANIEL No. I'm a dick.

NADIA   A cock.

DANIEL A prick.

NADIA   A big flaccid one.

DANIEL The worst kind.

NADIA   Exactly.

DANIEL I don't want to share you either.

(*A beat, she smiles.*)

NADIA   So it's boring monogamy?

DANIEL Terribly boring, extra-marital, monogamy.

(*Pause.*)

Have you ever… Before. This. Us.

NADIA   Have I ever what?

DANIEL Done this. Before. Am I your first?

NADIA   Yes, I am in fact a virgin and my children were actually given to me by an angel called Gabriel. It's a well-known phenomenon.

DANIEL *Nadia*.

NADIA   Of course not. This is special. Us. We're special.

(*Pause.*)

Now let's stop talking.

DANIEL Why?

NADIA   It's overrated.

(*She places her hand hard on* DANIEL*'s throat and pushes him down to the floor.*)

3.

(*The curtains are open and light floods into the space.*

NADIA stands by the windows. DANIEL crouches in the middle of the room. A moment. Then…)

NADIA   We need to get some furniture. Some throws.

(*She looks at the mattress.*)

Sheets. Some things to makes it less –

DANIEL   Squalid.

NADIA   I was going to say plain.

(*Beat.*)

It needs to look normal. Like people live here.

DANIEL   People do live here.

NADIA   You know what I mean. In case someone comes.

DANIEL   Are we expecting guests?

NADIA   If the landlord wants to visit.

DANIEL   *Or pops round for tea.*

(*Beat.*)

Do we even have tea?

NADIA   Yes.

DANIEL   Real tea?

NADIA   Green tea is real tea.

DANIEL   I don't think he'll see it that way. In fact, nobody does. Except you.

NADIA   I'm the exception.

DANIEL   Yes, yes you are.

(*Pause.*)

I could order some stuff. From Ikea.

NADIA   Ikea?

DANIEL Yeah.

NADIA   I'll pick up some things.

DANIEL What's wrong with Ikea?

NADIA   Daniel.

DANIEL *A woman's touch.*

(*She laughs.*)

What's funny?

NADIA   I didn't realise you were one of those.

DANIEL *One of those* what?

NADIA   Wankers.

DANIEL Make sure you pay / cash.

NADIA   Cash. I know. We've been through this a million times.

DANIEL I don't mean to be boring, this is just important. There's no need to take unnecessary risks.

(NADIA *has moved to her coat and bag.*)

NADIA   I've actually been meaning to give you something.

DANIEL I thought we said no moving-in presents?

(*She takes out a piece of paper. Hands it to him.*)

'*The Rules*'. It's got a little title and everything.

NADIA   Yes it has.

DANIEL There's ten of them.

NADIA   Yup.

DANIEL In bold.

NADIA   Underlined.

DANIEL Stop, you're getting me hard.

NADIA   Times New Roman.

DANIEL Serious then. Not sexy.

NADIA   Serious can be sexy.

         (*He holds it to the side, reaches for her.*)

         Daniel, please. Read it.

         (*He reads it.*)

DANIEL   Read.

NADIA   Do you want to add anything?

DANIEL   Looks like you've got it all covered.

NADIA   You're not taking this seriously.

         (*He smiles.*)

DANIEL   No.

NADIA   I just want to make sure we don't –

DANIEL   Get caught?

         (*Beat.*)

NADIA   I've got responsibilities.

DANIEL   We both have.

NADIA   Children.

DANIEL   We're both parents.

NADIA   People don't think that way though, do they? It's worse if you are –

DANIEL   A woman?

NADIA   Yes.

DANIEL   A mother?

NADIA   Yes. Yes, it actually is.

DANIEL   Says who?

NADIA   Everyone.

DANIEL   And because everyone says it, it must be true?

NADIA   In this case, yes.

DANIEL   Did you write this at home? In your house?

NADIA   Yes, but –

DANIEL   Where *your children* live?

NADIA   Let's not make this into –

DANIEL   Did you delete it after?

NADIA   Of course I did.

DANIEL   And the recycle bin?

NADIA   Yes.

DANIEL   And the lists of printed documents?

NADIA   Yes.

DANIEL   Because you know they still show up even after you delete the file?

NADIA   I'm not an idiot, Daniel.

DANIEL   No. You're a mother. A mother with your *responsibilities*. What do you think happens if your husband found it? If he tells someone? You think I'll get to see my kids as much as you would after a divorce? You think that's the way it fucking works when it comes to custody battles?

(She moves closer to him. Touches his hand; a peace offering.)

NADIA   Daniel…

DANIEL   Sorry. I didn't mean to… I'm new at this.

A silence.

NADIA   I deleted the files. I know I did. I wouldn't be that careless.

DANIEL   It's fine. Why would he look? Why would he be suspicious?

NADIA   I was just trying to… Make it formal. Us. Make it more than just –

DANIEL   We don't need a list to do that.

      (*He looks at 'The Rules' again.*)

      Have you got a pen?

      (*She rummages in her bag. Passes him a pen.*)

      Rule number eleven: We don't talk about them. Not here. They don't exist here.

      (*Beat.*)

NADIA   Eleven... One better than god.

4.

(*The mattress now sits on a divan base. There is a table next to it. A couple of throws have been placed around the room. A lightshade on the bare bulb.*

DANIEL *is lying on the bed reading a paper. The sound of the shower can be heard from off.*

DANIEL*'s phone starts to ring. He picks it up from the table. Silences it.*

NADIA *comes into the room wearing a white dressing gown. She dries her hair with a towel. She speaks in a Russian accent. Hamming it up fully.*)

NADIA   *Would you like some breakfast?*

      (DANIEL *replies in his normal voice.*)

DANIEL   It's nearly dark.

NADIA   *Well, that is a disappointment.*

DANIEL   Do we have to?

NADIA   *Da.*

DANIEL   I feel like a dick.

(*She drops out of the accent.*)

NADIA   Pretend. If you practise, it'll get better.

DANIEL   You have too much faith in me.

NADIA   You don't have enough.

(*Pause.*)

Haven't you ever wanted to be someone else?

DANIEL   Constantly.

NADIA   Then try.

(*Beat, and back to it.*)

Would you like some breakfast?

(*He tries the accent. It's bad.*)

DANIEL   *If it's not too much trouble.*

(*She smiles.*)

NADIA   *In bed?*

DANIEL   *Why not.*

NADIA   *Excellent.*

(*Beat.*)

DANIEL   I can't. I just can't do it. I feel like an idiot. Feeling like an idiot is not sexy.

(NADIA *drops the accent.*)

NADIA   Neither is being boring.

(*She wanders into the kitchen. We hear her from off.*)

What's in the paper?

DANIEL   Sport.

NADIA   The real paper?

DANIEL   Debt. Death. Genocide. But not here. So don't fret.

NADIA   You are such a heathen.

DANIEL   That's why you love me.

(She walks back into the room. Without breakfast.)

Breakfast?

NADIA   Rule number one. The L-word. We don't do that.
That's what normal people do.

DANIEL   I didn't –

NADIA   They say it, they say it all the time, and so it means
nothing. *We're not those kind of people. Are we?*

*(She blows him a kiss as she exits back into the
kitchen.*

We hear her throughout the next exchange from off.)

DANIEL   We should have a substitute.

NADIA   A substitute?

DANIEL   Word. For that which we shall never say. The curse.

NADIA   Okay. Like what?

(Pause.)

DANIEL   Sport.

NADIA   I sport you?

DANIEL   Get back in here then.

NADIA   Funny you should say that, as I'm actually in the
mood for a bit of sport.

*(DANIEL gets up and rushes into the kitchen. The
sound of laughter from off.*

Moments pass.

DANIEL *and* NADIA *return into the room. They
both have plates loaded with toast. They sit on
the bed.)*

DANIEL   Could get used to this. When I'm at home I'm not
allowed toast in bed.

(NADIA *picks up a piece of toast from his plate and stuffs it in his mouth.* DANIEL *tries to speak but can't. He makes a big show of finishing his mouthful. Glugs back some water.*)

NADIA   Punishment.

DANIEL   I nearly choked.

NADIA   Nearly.

DANIEL   You are cruel.

(NADIA *slips back into the accent for the following line.*)

NADIA   *You like me cruel.*

(*Beat.*)

Let's spend the night.

(*Pause.*)

DANIEL   We said –

NADIA   I know what we said. But this once.

DANIEL   We have rules. You printed them. There was a title and everything. Underlined.

NADIA   I know.

DANIEL   Then why would we –

NADIA   Because I want to have more.

DANIEL   More what?

NADIA   More time. More this. More you.

(*Pause.*)

You can say no. It's okay. I understand.

DANIEL   I'm sorry.

NADIA   Don't be. I shouldn't have said anything.

DANIEL   I want to.

NADIA   It's fine.

DANIEL   I do.

NADIA   Let's talk about something else.

DANIEL   I just can't just lie about work like you. I work in a shop.

NADIA   You fix clocks.

DANIEL   And?

NADIA   Find some time then.

DANIEL   Nadia.

NADIA   You go away on courses.

DANIEL   Conventions.

NADIA   Sounds hot.

DANIEL   It is.

NADIA   Never know who you will meet in those hotel bars.

DANIEL   You.

NADIA   Perhaps a convention might have just come up. Unexpectedly.

(*Pause*.)

DANIEL   They are on the family calendar. They are planned.

NADIA   In your little house.

DANIEL   Yes. The calendar in my *little* house. In the kitchen.

NADIA   How homely. How quaint.

(*A silence*.)

That was cruel.

DANIEL   A little.

NADIA   Sorry.

DANIEL   It's fine.

NADIA   I was just jealous. For a second. Ugly isn't it? Cliché.

(*Beat*.)

You hate me now, don't you? I can see it in your eyes.

(*He leans in to her and whispers something inaudible in her ear, a wide smile crosses her face.*

His phone starts to vibrate, breaking the moment.)

Turn it off.

DANIEL   How am I going to tell her I've got to work late if I do that.

(*She smiles. Picks up his phone. It continues to vibrate.*)

NADIA   Late?

DANIEL   Could be an all-nighter. Not worth the journey home. Might stay round Steve's.

NADIA   Steve?

DANIEL   From work. He lives close to the shop. Makes sense.

(*She hands him the phone.*)

NADIA   *Lucky Steve.*

5.

(NADIA *is standing on the small table. Music plays from an iPod. Think 'Love is a Stranger' by Eurythmics, etc.*

She dances.

DANIEL *stands watching.*)

DANIEL   Come down.

NADIA   Why should I?

DANIEL   You're drunk.

NADIA   And?

DANIEL   You might fall. Hurt yourself.

NADIA   It's my table.

DANIEL   Actually...

NADIA   It's *our* table. In *our* flat. So if I want to stand on it, I will.

DANIEL   I take it the meeting went well?

NADIA   Very well.

DANIEL   Maybe we could upsize.

NADIA   This place not good enough for you?

DANIEL   No spare bedrooms. For the kids.

NADIA   Funny.

DANIEL   Come down.

NADIA   Come up.

         (*A moment. Stalemate. He does.*)

         See. Isn't that nicer?

DANIEL   It's definitely higher.

         (*She kisses him.*)

         What was that for?

NADIA   Because I could.

DANIEL   Can we get down now?

NADIA   No.

DANIEL   Okay.

NADIA   We can do anything we want.

DANIEL   Except get down off the –

NADIA   Why do we make everything so small? So safe.
What's the point?

DANIEL   Exactly. Let's all stand on tables.

          (*She places a finger on his lips.*)

NADIA   Shhhh.

DANIEL   I am shushed.

NADIA   Look out of the window.

DANIEL   I can't actually look out of it, unless I get –

NADIA   LOOK!

          (*He makes a big gesture of looking in the direction of
          the window.*)

          Everyone is just sat there in their little boxes.
          Trapped. Meet someone at twenty pissed in some shit
          bar. Six months of good sex, then it's just '*What true
          crime show shall we watch next on Netflix?*' '*The one
          with the staircase?*', '*Sounds great*', '*Aren't we
          cultured*', '*I bet he did it*'. WHO. FUCKING.
          CARES. The occasional fumble. The occasional
          night of physical fucking contact when neither of you
          can be bothered to even say you're too tired.

DANIEL   I'm wide awake –

NADIA   '*Let's get married! Nice excuse to see everyone
          again. Fill a weekend.*' Then that's it for the rest of
          your life isn't it? Filling weekends.

DANIEL   And?

NADIA   It's just all so fucking boring!

          (*Beat.*)

          I want more than that.

DANIEL   You can have more.

NADIA   Can I?

DANIEL   Yes.

          (*Pause.*)

          You just have to get divorced first.

NADIA   And what then? You and me? Tie the knot. Nice
          white dress. You in a tux?

DANIEL   I look shit in a tux.

NADIA   Repeat it again. And again. And again. Fuck
          marriage. Fuck monogamy. Why can't we all just be
          what we want? Do what we want? All the time.
          What's so wrong with that?

          (*A moment.*)

DANIEL   You mean get drunk at two in the afternoon?

NADIA   Yeah.

DANIEL   Stand on tables and listen to music from the eighties?

NADIA   Yeah, why fucking not?

DANIEL   I'm sober.

NADIA   Well that, my sweet, is a character flaw.

          (NADIA *points sharply to the kitchen.*)

          Go to the kitchen.

DANIEL   So I can get down now?

NADIA   Yes. But only to go to the kitchen. Then you have to
          get back up. Go. Quickly.

          (*He gets down and exits to the kitchen. Then enters
          with a bottle of vodka.*)

          Well?

DANIEL   What?

(*She gives him a look.*)

Oh.

(*He gets back on the table. Undoes the lid of the bottle. Drinks from it. Gags slightly.*)

NADIA   Pussy.

(*She takes the bottle back and drinks. Long. Hard.*)

DANIEL   You said you had to go back tonight.

NADIA   Don't be boring.

DANIEL   I'm just trying to be / practical.

NADIA   *Practical.*

DANIEL   Yes.

NADIA   I don't want you to be practical.

DANIEL   What do you want me to do then?

(*She kisses him, hard, felt.*

The bottle slips from her grasp and smashes on the floor.)

Fuck.

NADIA   Leave it.

DANIEL   Nadia, there's glass everywhere.

NADIA   Fuck it. Stay here. Stay here with me.

(*He looks to the floor.*)

DANIEL   Let me just…

(*He gets down and carefully starts to move towards the kitchen.*

NADIA *hops down from the table and walks after him.*)

NADIA   Ow.

(*She's bleeding. Quite profusely.* DANIEL *turns on her noise. Sees the blood.*)

DANIEL Are you okay?

>(*She puts her foot back down on the floor, the broken glass.*)

Don't.

>(*She takes another step.*)

Nadia…

>(*She continues towards him across the broken glass, leaving a trail of bloody footprints. He takes her into his arms.*)

6.

(DANIEL *sits on the floor. He taps at his phone.*

He starts to pace the room.

Sits. Checks his phone again.

The sound of a key in the front door. It opens to reveal NADIA. *She smiles seeing* DANIEL *there, enters.*)

NADIA Thank god, I thought you might have left.

DANIEL We said twelve o'clock.

NADIA I text.

DANIEL I know.

NADIA I wanted to –

DANIEL Call? No communication outside the flat. Rule number three. Your rule.

NADIA I know, but –

DANIEL Your child is ill.

NADIA My son.

DANIEL Your youngest. Just starting nursery. It's a tricky time.

NADIA   It is actually.

DANIEL   I remember how much it upset my wife.

NADIA   Why are you bringing her –

DANIEL   Abandoning them, that's what she used to call it. Abandoning your children at the nursery. Palming them off. Giving them to someone else to raise. Of course, it's not the same for you and your husband, is it?

NADIA   Daniel.

DANIEL   With your nannies and your help and your –

NADIA   You really have no fucking idea what you're talking about, so why don't you stop speaking before you say something you will regret.

(NADIA *enters the room and shuts the door. Takes a breath. Smiles.*

She takes her shoes off and comes and sits down on DANIEL*'s lap.*)

Can we be friends again?

DANIEL   I'm not in the mood.

NADIA   Maybe I know something that will –

(DANIEL *stands up.*)

DANIEL   I said I'm not in the mood.

NADIA   What's wrong? I came. It was really fucking difficult, but I still came. I'm here now.

DANIEL   Yes. You are. With all your...

(*Beat.*)

Fuck it. It doesn't matter.

NADIA   All my what?

DANIEL   *Nothing.*

NADIA   You obviously want to say something. So say it.

(*Beat.*)

If I wanted to have some passive-aggressive bullshit
row, I could have just stayed at home.

DANIEL With all your *stuff*.

NADIA What *stuff*?

DANIEL Your child, your nursery, your husband. Your life.
Your other life.

NADIA You mentioned my husband not me. *Your rule*. By
the way.

(*Pause*.)

My son was sick.

DANIEL You think my children never get ill?

NADIA Why are you being so –

DANIEL Answer me.

NADIA I don't know.

DANIEL Exactly. You don't know. And you know why you
don't know?

NADIA No. But I'm pretty sure you're going to tell me.

DANIEL Because I don't bring that kind of thing here. Not on
Mondays. Because that time is meant to mean
something. Isn't it? That's what we said.

(*A silence*.)

NADIA Are you finished?

DANIEL Yes.

(DANIEL *takes out a gift bag*.)

NADIA What's that?

DANIEL Happy anniversary.

(*Pause*.)

One year.

NADIA We haven't –

DANIEL Since we moved in. Yes. We have.

NADIA   It can't be.

DANIEL   It is. Time. I'm good with time. Open it.

NADIA   I don't deserve a present.

DANIEL   I can't take it back. I paid / cash.

NADIA   Cash.

(*She smiles at him. It's infectious.*)

So I'm stuck with it then.

(*She opens the bag. Takes a small box from it. Opens the box. It's an old pocket watch.*

She holds it up to the light.)

It's beautiful.

DANIEL   I know.

(*Beat.*)

I'm sorry.

NADIA   It's not your fault.

DANIEL   I just wanted everything to be perfect.

NADIA   It is.

DANIEL   I even cooked.

NADIA   Really?

DANIEL   The food was lovely, actually.

NADIA   Ah, but you have such low standards.

DANIEL   I know.

NADIA   Where's mine?

DANIEL   I was hungry.

NADIA   And angry?

(*Beat.*)

Hangry.

(*They both smile.*)

DANIEL Had to force it down.

NADIA I am sorry. Really.

(*Beat*.)

DANIEL Is he okay?

NADIA You don't have to ask.

DANIEL I'm not a monster.

NADIA I know.

DANIEL Just because we're doing this doesn't mean we're monsters.

(*Pause*.)

Is he –

NADIA He's fine.

DANIEL And you?

NADIA Better. Now I'm better.

7.

(NADIA *is drinking a glass of wine*.

DANIEL *sits with a phone in his hands*.)

DANIEL *A burner?*

NADIA That's what the kids call them.

DANIEL I already have a phone.

NADIA I know that.

DANIEL What happens if my / wife –

NADIA She who will not be named.

DANIEL What happens if *she who will not be named* finds it?

NADIA   Don't let her. Simple.

DANIEL   Well obviously I won't deliberately let her find it.
          But even so –

NADIA   Don't you want to be able to talk more?

          (*Beat.*)

DANIEL   When you say talk…

NADIA   There may be pictures as well.

DANIEL   Sold.

NADIA   There are some rules though.

DANIEL   You do love a set of rules.

NADIA   Without rules this doesn't work.

DANIEL   A phone is quite clearly contravening –

NADIA   Things change.

          (*He smiles.*)

DANIEL   Do they?

NADIA   Yes. But that doesn't mean we can get sloppy. That's
          why we have safeguards in place.

DANIEL   Safeguards. Hot. Please continue.

NADIA   We use a stock phrase to find out if it's a good time
          before engaging.

DANIEL   A code.

NADIA   If you like.

DANIEL   *Sport.*

NADIA   Not fucking *sport*.

DANIEL   I thought you liked *fucking sport*?

NADIA   It amused me.

DANIEL   *Amused*. That's damning.

          (*Beat.*)

          Well what is your non-amusing alternative then?

NADIA   '*Are you free?*'

DANIEL   That's the best you've got?

NADIA   Gets to the point pretty well I thought.

DANIEL   You are so efficient.

NADIA   This isn't a game, Daniel.

DANIEL   I know that.

NADIA   Then stop taking the piss!

DANIEL   If I knew sexting was so important to you, I –

NADIA   Don't say *sexting*. It makes you sound ancient.

DANIEL   That's what it's called.

NADIA   I know what it's called.

DANIEL   Then –

NADIA   For fucksake. I was just… I…

          (*Pause.*)

          If something happened to you…

DANIEL   Like what?

NADIA   An emergency.

DANIEL   What kind of emergency?

NADIA   You get hit by a car. I get hit by a car. A bomb goes off and wipes out half of London. An emergency.

DANIEL   Then what? With my dying breath I text you?

NADIA   Call. You call me.

DANIEL   Might be difficult if it's nuclear.

NADIA   I'll take it back to the shop.

DANIEL   Nadia.

NADIA   It was a stupid idea.

DANIEL   No. It wasn't.

NADIA   I just…

        (*Beat, she laughs.*)

        I just had this thought the other day… I'm being crazy. Ignore me.

DANIEL   What thought?

NADIA   How small this is.

DANIEL   It's not small. Not to me.

NADIA   To everyone else… All the people that care about me. They don't even know you exist.

DANIEL   They can't.

NADIA   I know that.

        (*Beat.*)

DANIEL   But I can call you. From now. *On my burner.*

NADIA   Can you?

DANIEL   Yes, I can.

NADIA   Even if there's a nuclear bomb?

DANIEL   Yes.

NADIA   Even if you get hit by a car?

DANIEL   It will be the last thing I do.

NADIA   And what will you say?

        (*Pause.*)

DANIEL   *Send me a picture of your tits.*

        (*She laughs.*)

NADIA   And I shall.

        (DANIEL *types a message into the phone. Presses send.*

        NADIA*'s phone makes a noise. She picks it up. Reads the message.*)

        Daniel…

DANIEL   An exception. This once.

(*She puts a hand to his face.*

They hold each other.)

8.

(DANIEL *is by the window. He peeks a look outside through the closed curtains.*

NADIA *enters eating a packet of crisps.*)

DANIEL   She's still out there.

NADIA   Why are you whispering?

DANIEL   Why would she be here?

NADIA   I don't know. Open the window. Ask her.

DANIEL   If it was one of your people –

NADIA   One of my people?

DANIEL   You know what I mean.

NADIA   My *people*.

DANIEL   You *know* what I <u>mean</u>.

NADIA   Yes, I do. And if it was one of *my people*, I would shut the curtains and come and sit down. Possibly take off some clothes.

DANIEL   What a lovely, hypothetical, reaction that is.

NADIA   She hasn't followed you.

DANIEL   I didn't say she… What?! Why would she… My wife is stood in the street outside the flat where –

NADIA   Your fuck pad.

DANIEL   *Our* fuck pad.

NADIA   I'm glad we finally came up with a name for the place.

          (*He takes one more look through the curtains*.)

          Come away from the window. Please.

          (*He does*.)

          She would have knocked if she followed you. You don't follow someone all the way out here and then stop in the street. You'd knock on the door.

DANIEL   We don't have a knocker.

NADIA   Ring the bell then. Ring you on your phone. Text. Try and communicate in some way. She wouldn't just stand outside in the street.

DANIEL   I'm just being paranoid.

NADIA   Yes.

DANIEL   It's just this is... I just didn't think it would make me feel like this.

NADIA   Like what?

DANIEL   Sick.

          (*A silence*.)

          Can you check to see whether she's gone?

NADIA   That's what you want?

          (*He nods*.)

          What you really, really want?

DANIEL   Don't fuck around. Just look. Please.

          (NADIA *opens the curtain. She shuts it quickly. Gasps*.)

          What?

          (*She shakes her head*.)

          What?!

NADIA   Okay. Sit down.

DANIEL   Just fucking tell me, Nadia.

        (*Pause.*)

NADIA   She's with a man.

DANIEL   A man?

NADIA   They just kissed.

        (DANIEL *gets up and rushes to the window throwing open the curtain.* NADIA *stifles a laugh.*)

DANIEL   You lied.

NADIA   I did.

DANIEL   There's no man.

NADIA   No.

DANIEL   She's shopping.

NADIA   I know.

DANIEL   She has bags and –

NADIA   She looks happy.

DANIEL   Why would you –

NADIA   Because.

        (*He shakes his head. Walks towards where his coat and bag has been thrown on the floor.*)

        Because you were being insane. Impossible. No fun. And today is meant to be about fun.

        (*He puts his coat on and starts towards the door.*)

        Your wife. Outside. Remember.

        (*He stops.*)

        Why shouldn't she have a man? You have me. Why shouldn't she have someone?

DANIEL   She's not like that.

        (*Beat.*)

NADIA   *She's not like that.*

DANIEL   I didn't mean –

NADIA   But I am? Is that it?

DANIEL   Don't try and make me seem like the bad guy. You are complicit. In fact, if I remember correctly, you were the one who –

NADIA   What if we tell them?

(*Pause.*)

And we tell them it's not just about us. Maybe they feel like we did too. Maybe they just never acted on it. It doesn't mean we don't care about them. It doesn't mean anything has to end. They could have someone else as well if they want. And it wouldn't matter. Not if we were honest with each other.

(*Beat.*)

We tell them the truth.

DANIEL   And?

NADIA   And we could just be happy. Actually happy.

(*Pause.*)

Look at your scared little eyes.

(*A silence.*)

DANIEL   Shall we have some tea?

NADIA   That is quite possibly the most English thing I think anyone has ever said.

DANIEL   I just… I just need a cup of tea. Okay.

NADIA   Okay.

(*He walks through into the kitchen.* NADIA *gets up and walks over to the window. She opens the curtains. The room is flooded with light. She shuts them again.*

DANIEL *enters with two cups of tea. Sits down next to* NADIA.)

DANIEL   So...

NADIA   I –

DANIEL   Don't. Let me say this. Out loud.

NADIA   Okay. Sorry. Speak.

DANIEL   We break up both our marriages. Break up two families. Possibly fuck up our relationships with our kids.

NADIA   I didn't say that.

DANIEL   Destroy ourselves financially. That. That is what you are saying. Right? Just so I can be clear on this. Because out there, in the real world, if I tell my wife what you just said –

NADIA   Why does it have to be like that?

(*Pause.*)

She is out there. Shopping. Happy. We are in here. Together. Happy. If we were just honest about it... If we all just told the fucking truth for once in our lives... The real truth. Why is that sick?

(*Beat.*)

I'm just saying perhaps we should talk about this. Really talk about it.

(*Pause.*)

DANIEL   Okay. Let's talk about it.

9.

(*The sheets are pulled off the mattress and lie next to it in a bundle. NADIA and DANIEL are to the side of them. She is wearing her coat.*)

NADIA   I did ask. I made a point of asking.

DANIEL   You did.

NADIA   And it's not the first time. I don't complain. I don't. Don't look at me like I do. I just asked you, specifically, this time.

DANIEL   And I apologised. Profusely.

NADIA   But that isn't going to magic the sheets clean now is it?

DANIEL   Then let's have a day without sheets on the bed. The world will not end. And we can move on from –

NADIA   It's a divan. Not a bed.

DANIEL   And?

NADIA   We've had this place for a year and a half and we don't even have a proper bed.

DANIEL   We have throws.

NADIA   I know. I bought them.

DANIEL   We have a table.

NADIA   You stole from your work.

DANIEL   And brought here. On the Central line. In rush hour, no less.

NADIA   I don't want to sleep on a dirty mattress.

DANIEL   The table is pretty sturdy.

(*A silence.*)

NADIA   I might go home.

DANIEL   Okay.

(*Pause.*)

NADIA   Okay?

DANIEL   Yes. Okay.

NADIA   You are such a fucking...

DANIEL   What? A fucking what?

NADIA   It's just temporary isn't it? This. Us. Everything.
           Your whole fucking life.

DANIEL   Well, yes, actually. Life is just temporary. All life.
           Not just mine. Not just yours. Every living –

NADIA   Thank you very much, Jean-Paul-fucking-Sartre.

           (*Beat.*)

DANIEL   You said –

NADIA   Here we go.

DANIEL   You were the one. When we spoke. You said –

NADIA   Stop saying that.

DANIEL   But you did, didn't you? When we spoke. I said I was
           happy to, but you... *After careful and considered
           thought.* You –

NADIA   I swear to god if you say it again.

DANIEL   *If we can just wait a couple of years. Till they are at
           big school.*

NADIA   Daniel.

DANIEL   Was that right?

NADIA   Stop.

DANIEL   The tone? Was the tone right? I'm sure the words
           were. I can remember you saying *big school* and
           thinking it was either sweet or fucking retarded. But
           maybe my tone was off? What do you think?

NADIA   Now.

DANIEL   Okay. Fuck tone. Regardless of tone. I said let's do it.
           Let's fucking do it. You and me. Fuck everyone else.

Fuck the repercussions. Fuck who we hurt. And
you… You *coward*… You just said –

(NADIA *screams*.)

Somewhat of an overreaction.

NADIA   I'm late.

DANIEL   For what?

NADIA   Registering to vote. What do you fucking think?

(*A silence*.)

DANIEL   How late?

NADIA   Late enough.

DANIEL   Late enough to what? Go to the doctor's? Tell a friend?
Order a cot?

NADIA   We couldn't even order a bed.

DANIEL   A cot would be easier to carry on the Tube.

NADIA   Late.

(*Pause*.)

DANIEL   Is it mine?

(*Beat*.)

NADIA   I can't believe you just said that.

DANIEL   I think in the circumstances it's –

NADIA   Stop. Talking.

(*A silence*.)

DANIEL   I don't… With her… Any more. I'm not saying that
you have to do the same with your husband. That
I want you to. And I didn't want to ask if you still
did. I didn't –

NADIA   It's yours.

(*He moves to her. A moment between them*.)

DANIEL   And do you feel…

NADIA   Yes.

          (*Slowly,* NADIA *starts to smile.*)

          Yes I do feel… It.

10.

(*The curtains are open and light floods into the flat.* NADIA
and DANIEL *are sat around the small table.*)

NADIA   You will still fuck me, after.

DANIEL   Fuck?

NADIA   Yes.

DANIEL   Make love.

NADIA   That's a euphemism for bad sex, isn't it?

          (DANIEL *laughs.*)

          I'm serious. That's what happens. I should know.
          You see the business end being used for what it's
          actually meant for and you go limp. Men.

DANIEL   Have no fear, for I shall be sturdy.

NADIA   Good. What use are you to me otherwise?

DANIEL   You are so alpha.

NADIA   Someone has to be in this relationship.

          (*She kisses him.*)

DANIEL   When are you going to tell him?

NADIA   Soon. You?

DANIEL   Same.

NADIA   What do you think she'll say?

DANIEL   I don't know.

          (*Pause.*)

NADIA   I imagine her sometimes. Her voice. How she treats you. How you met. Your secrets.

DANIEL   You're my secret.

NADIA   Not for much longer.

(*She touches his hand.*)

Do you? Wonder what he's like? My husband.

DANIEL   No.

NADIA   Never?

DANIEL   I don't want to think about that. I want you all for myself.

NADIA   How greedy.

DANIEL   I'm insatiable.

NADIA   You are.

(*Pause.*)

DANIEL   She either understands. Or she divorces me. Whatever happens, I'm not giving this up. Us.

NADIA   I think he'll shout. Men like to shout.

DANIEL   It's a male trait.

NADIA   It really is.

DANIEL   And then?

NADIA   Probably call me some names.

DANIEL   What ones?

NADIA   Slut.

DANIEL   Ouch.

NADIA   Slag.

DANIEL   What a loser.

NADIA   Then he'll bring out the big guns.

DANIEL   Yeah?

NADIA   *Whore. You fucking whore.*

DANIEL   I've never paid you.

NADIA   You couldn't afford me.

DANIEL   I know.

          (*Pause.*)

          No more nuclear family.

NADIA   When has anything with the word nuclear ever been good?

DANIEL   People will speak.

NADIA   People are afraid.

DANIEL   And you're not?

NADIA   No. No I'm not.

DANIEL   Your family?

NADIA   They're my family. Families accept things. Move on.

DANIEL   It's going to be okay isn't it?

NADIA   Yes. I think it is.

DANIEL   No more lies. No more working late. No more *Steve.*

NADIA   Shame. The name was really starting to grow on me.

          (NADIA *moves to her coat and retrieves something.*)

          I know I shouldn't have… It's too soon… I just saw this the other day and…

          (*She passes it to* DANIEL. *It's a small, ornate, children's music box.*)

DANIEL   It's perfect. You're perfect.

          (*A moment. Then* NADIA *laughs to herself.*)

          What's funny?

NADIA   This. Us. No one suspected. It wasn't even hard.

DANIEL   You did rent us a flat.

NADIA   I did, but… It's almost like people didn't want to see.
          They're just so busy lying to themselves to get
          through the day. '*Look, here's a picture of us on
          holiday!*' '*Look how happy we are.*' '*Aren't we
          happy?*' Liars. They're just killing time.

          (*Pause.*)

DANIEL   Speaking of time, have we…

NADIA   Again?

DANIEL   Want to make use of the business end, you know,
          before it's ruined.

          (*She slaps him playfully.*)

11.

(*Night.*

The room is dark.

NADIA *is in a dressing gown in the bed. She has the duvet
wrapped round her.*

The sound of a key in the lock. DANIEL *enters. He sees*
NADIA. *Moves to her. Holds her for some time.*)

DANIEL   I'm sorry. I came as soon as I could. It's just /
          Sunday.

NADIA   Sunday. I understand.

DANIEL   When did… Why didn't you call me?

NADIA   I wanted to go to the doctor first.

DANIEL   And?

          (*She shakes her head.*

          Silence.)

NADIA   I don't want to go home.

DANIEL You don't have to.

NADIA   I do.

DANIEL Give me your phone. I'll text him. Make up an
        excuse.

NADIA   It's...

        (*She laughs. Sad. Desperate.*)

        It's my son's birthday.

        (*A silence.*)

        I could only get away for an hour. I just wanted to
        see you. To be... This.

DANIEL Tomorrow. We'll stay here then. Together. The whole
        night.

        (*Pause.*)

        This doesn't change anything.

NADIA   It just made me think... And I can't look at myself
        now. I can't physically look at my own reflection...
        How could a mother...

        (*Pause.*)

        Maybe this was for the best.

DANIEL Nadia...

NADIA   Maybe we deserve this.

        (*They sit in silence.*)

DANIEL We can try again.

        (*Beat.*)

NADIA   I need to get ready. I can't go home like this.

DANIEL Then stay.

        (*She stands and walks towards the bathroom. The
        sound of the shower can be heard.*)

12.

(DANIEL *and* NADIA *are sat on the floor. Around them are the plastic containers of a takeaway meal. A half-bottle of red wine.*)

NADIA   Do you want to take it for later? The leftovers?

DANIEL   No, I'm good.

NADIA   For *Steve*?

              (*He smiles. Sad. Knowing.*)

              Seems a waste.

              (*Pause.*)

              It was nice. You did enjoy it?

DANIEL   Yes.

NADIA   Not too spicy?

DANIEL   No.

NADIA   I preferred yours.

DANIEL   I saw.

NADIA   Thank you for sharing.

              (*Beat.*)

              I'm glad we could do this. Together. Be like this.

DANIEL   And so… This place, the lease?

NADIA   I'll sort something out.

DANIEL   We must still have, what, five months?

NADIA   Four.

DANIEL   I'd like to help with the rent.

              (*Beat.*)

              I could give you some / cash.

NADIA   Cash?

DANIEL   Maybe in instalments.

NADIA   It's fine.

DANIEL   Or send it through your friend. The *sympathiser.*

NADIA   She still asks after you.

DANIEL   And what do you say?

NADIA   Not a lot. What is there to say any more?

(DANIEL *stands*.)

Are you okay?

DANIEL   Yes.

(*He paces*.)

No.

NADIA   Come here.

DANIEL   I don't think that's going to help.

NADIA   Tell me what is? Anything. I don't want this to end like –

(*He laughs. Shakes his head*.)

What?

DANIEL   The way you're talking.

NADIA   How would you like me to talk?

DANIEL   I'd like you to not be so fucking polite about everything. Like this is the end of one of your fucking business meetings. Like this didn't mean anything.

NADIA   It did mean something.

DANIEL   It meant something to me.

NADIA   I can't do this again.

DANIEL   You've said. Funny how we change, isn't it?

NADIA   I had to choose.

DANIEL   And you chose him.

NADIA   Them. My children.

(*A silence*.)

DANIEL I'm sorry. I didn't want to be like this.

NADIA   You don't have to apologise.

DANIEL I do. I asked you to come and you have. You did this for me. And now I'm acting like a prick.

(*Pause.*)

NADIA   A cock.

DANIEL A dick.

NADIA   Are you flirting with me?

DANIEL Always.

(*Beat.*)

Will you ever tell him?

(NADIA *laughs*.)

You can never be innocent again.

NADIA   I'm an adult, Daniel. He wasn't the first man I fucked. You weren't the second.

DANIEL I love you.

NADIA   That's not a particularly helpful thing to say at this moment.

DANIEL It's the truth.

NADIA   '*The truth*'.

DANIEL Don't sneer.

NADIA   I'm not.

DANIEL Yes. You are.

NADIA   What good is the truth? You want me to go and tell your wife the truth?

DANIEL We used to talk –

NADIA   Fantasise. Not talk. That's all it was. This whole thing is a fantasy. A lovely, beautiful, one-day-a-week, good-while-it-lasted, fantasy. And I've been trying as much as I can to do this in a kind way. To not hurt you. Because I care about you. I really do. But it's over.

(*A silence.*)

DANIEL   A takeaway Chinese.

NADIA   You suggested Chinese.

(DANIEL *puts his coat on.*)

DANIEL   Sorry. About that. I don't know what came over me.

NADIA   You really don't have to apologise.

(DANIEL *is almost at the door. He stops.*)

DANIEL   I never thought I'd feel like this again. Butterflies… I actually feel nervous. Not nervous, anxious. Like this might be it. The end of my whole fucking life. Do you get that? Do you understand? I know it sounds crazy. I know.

NADIA   Daniel –

DANIEL   You get married and it's gone, isn't it? The end. Mortgage payments to think about instead. The kids' homework. The after-school clubs. '*Where should we go on holiday this year? Majorca?*' But us… We brought it back didn't we? We restarted it again. Mr and Mrs White.

(*She moves to him.*)

NADIA   *Majorca?*

DANIEL   I know.

(*A silence.*)

You don't love him.

NADIA   I do.

DANIEL   Not in the same way.

NADIA   I love my children.

DANIEL   I love my fucking children too, Nadia! That's not the… That's not…

(*Pause, he composes himself.*)

So how do we do this?

(NADIA *holds out her hand. Formal. Handshake.*)

I…

NADIA   I'm joking.

(*She grabs him. Holds him. For some time.*)

I will miss you.

DANIEL   Good.

(*She takes his hand. They exit.*)

13.

(*The room is empty.*

A long silence. Then…

A noise can be heard from the kitchen. It grows louder. Faster.

Breathing. Panting. Fucking.

It stops.

Moments pass.

DANIEL *enters the room and flops down on the bed.* NADIA *follows with a glass of water.*)

DANIEL   Well…

NADIA   Well.

DANIEL   That was nice.

NADIA   It was…

(*She laughs.*)

DANIEL   I wasn't bad, was I?

NADIA   Of course not!

         (*She moves to him on the bed. They kiss.*)

         It was just... different. From before. Ignore me. I'm a bit drunk.

DANIEL   Work drinks?

NADIA   Yeah.

DANIEL   Drink and dial?

NADIA   I'm a big girl. I know what I wanted.

DANIEL   And you got it?

NADIA   Yes. I did.

         (*Beat.*)

         I thought you'd be at home. When I text. I didn't actually think –

DANIEL   I was quick.

NADIA   Immediate.

DANIEL   Not too quick. Not / desperate –

NADIA   Oh, you're talking about –

DANIEL   Funny.

         (*Beat.*)

         It's been a while.

NADIA   Marital bliss.

DANIEL   Yeah.

NADIA   But you're happy?

DANIEL   You ever met someone post-coital who isn't?

NADIA   I meant –

DANIEL   I know what you meant.

(*They both lie back on the mattress. Breathe.*)

Do you have to go back? Tonight?

NADIA   No.

DANIEL   Do I?

(*Pause.*)

NADIA   No.

(DANIEL *stretches his arms out. Drops one around* NADIA. *The cliché noted.*)

DANIEL   Do you mind if I smoke? It's just it's a pain to get outside and I –

NADIA   You don't smoke.

(*He produces a packet of cigarettes from a pocket.*)

Well, that's going to change.

DANIEL   And what if I say no?

NADIA   I'll have to find another. A better. A non-smoker.

DANIEL   You witch.

(*Beat.*)

Didn't think you'd still have the place. I walk past sometimes. On my way home.

NADIA   I decided to keep it on.

DANIEL   Why?

NADIA   I don't know.

DANIEL   For your other men.

NADIA   My hordes of other men.

(*Beat.*)

This isn't on your way home.

DANIEL   It is.

NADIA   No. It's not.

DANIEL   It's not much of a detour.

NADIA   That's sweet.

DANIEL   Sad.

NADIA   Slightly sad. Stalkery.

DANIEL   I'd make a good stalker.

NADIA   You have got *that look*.

DANIEL   Intense?

NADIA   Alone. Needing to be saved.

DANIEL   Are you going to save me?

(*A silence.*)

14.

(*A small TV now sits on the table facing the bed.*)

NADIA   What the fuck is this?

DANIEL   It's called a television, I'm surprised you haven't
come across one before.

NADIA   Am I going to come back next time and find a fucking
pool table? A beer fridge?

DANIEL   A sex swing?

NADIA   Do you see me laughing? Do you?

DANIEL   Calm down.

NADIA   I am calm.

DANIEL   Calm people don't say that.

NADIA   If you want me to lose my temper –

DANIEL   Take a breath.

NADIA   *'Take a breath'?*

DANIEL   Let's start again.

NADIA   We've already done that, haven't we? Not working
          out so well at the moment.

DANIEL   Ouch.

NADIA   It's just every time I come here there seems to be
          more of –

DANIEL   Can we just let this go and actually spend some time
          together?

NADIA   I've got a TV at home.

DANIEL   It was just –

NADIA   What are we going to do? Curl up? Watch a movie?
          Catch up with fucking *Love Island*!

DANIEL   I don't know what *Love Island* is.

NADIA   Fuck!

DANIEL   I can find out if it's that important to you.

NADIA   Is that what this is now?

          (*A silence.*)

DANIEL   It was for when you weren't here.

NADIA   But you were. Right?

          (*Beat.*)

          I'm not going mental. I'm not that person. That's
          what is actually happening isn't it?

DANIEL   I've been doing some weird hours lately. It made
          sense to stay here.

NADIA   *'Weird hours'?*

DANIEL   Yeah.

NADIA   Am I your wife now?

DANIEL   No, I –

NADIA   Am I your fucking wife?

DANIEL   No.

NADIA   Then don't bullshit me. You work in a shop.

DANIEL I do repairs outside of office hours.

(*She points at the TV.*)

NADIA   Is that a clock?

DANIEL Can we calm this down a –

NADIA   Is that a fucking clock, Daniel?

DANIEL No.

NADIA   So where are all the clocks? If you've been working from here?

DANIEL I have fixed them.

NADIA   How dedicated of you.

(*He bows.*)

How long? Just tell me.

DANIEL You said I could stay.

NADIA   For a weekend. One weekend while your wife was away. I didn't say you can move in.

DANIEL I haven't moved in.

NADIA   Then why is your shit all over the flat.

DANIEL *Our shit.*

NADIA   Please just tell me how long.

(*Beat.*)

DANIEL A couple of weeks.

NADIA   Every night?

DANIEL A couple.

NADIA   That's not a number. How many nights have you stayed here?

(*Pause.*)

And what have you told her?

DANIEL I tell her I'm crashing at Steve's. Like I've always done.

NADIA   And she believes you? She buys that, does she?

DANIEL   I *have* got a lot of work on.

NADIA   Give me your key back.

DANIEL   What?

NADIA   Give me. Your key. Back.

DANIEL   Nadia…

NADIA   This is my flat.

DANIEL   Our flat.

NADIA   I don't remember you paying any money towards the rent.

DANIEL   Don't do that.

NADIA   It's the truth. How hard is it? We come here on Mondays. That's it. Then we go back to our lives.

DANIEL   I want more. More than Mondays.

NADIA   Well that's unfortunate.

DANIEL   Fuck you.

NADIA   No, fuck you.

DANIEL   I can't keep –

NADIA   Don't.

          (*Pause.*)

DANIEL   Before… When I didn't see you… It was like I couldn't breathe. Like I –

NADIA   You're with me now.

DANIEL   It's not the same.

NADIA   It's the same to me.

DANIEL   Liar.

          (*A silence.*)

          I'm keeping my key.

NADIA   Okay.

(*Beat*.)

But Daniel… Sort it out. I don't want to talk about this again.

(NADIA *starts to undress*.)

DANIEL   So that's it? You still want to –

NADIA   Of course. It's Monday. I've been looking forward to this all week.

15.

(*Night*.

NADIA *and* DANIEL *are laying on bed. The TV is still there. It plays lowly in the background*.)

DANIEL   You're asleep.

NADIA   I'm not.

DANIEL   Shall I turn it off?

NADIA   No. I want to see if he did it or not.

DANIEL   They won't say.

NADIA   How can you be sure?

DANIEL   Because there's another season.

NADIA   Maybe that's just about how happy he is after he gets out.

DANIEL   I can guarantee it's not.

NADIA   How?

DANIEL   Nobody wants to watch people being happy.

(*Pause*.)

Do you want to… After.

NADIA   What?

DANIEL   You know.

NADIA   I'm tired.

          (*Beat.*)

          It's not a thing. I'm just tired. I had a long day. I'm busy. Work.

DANIEL   It's fine.

          (*A silence.*)

NADIA   I'll make breakfast in the morning. Or we can get something out.

DANIEL   '*Out*'?

NADIA   Yeah. It's fine. We're just two people having breakfast. What's so wrong with that?

          (NADIA *rolls onto her side away from* DANIEL.)

DANIEL   I thought you were watching this?

NADIA   You've spoilt it now.

DANIEL   Do you want me to leave it on?

NADIA   Watch what you like.

          (DANIEL *takes the remote and changes the channel. He smiles.*)

DANIEL   There's some sport on.

          (*Beat.*)

          Sport.

NADIA   I'm just going to close my eyes for a bit.

          (*She does.*

          DANIEL *continues to watch the TV.*)

16.

(*Night.*

NADIA *sits alone in the room. The light from one candle all that illuminates her. The music box, from Scene Ten, is on the table with its lid open. A soft melody plays.*

She blows out the candle.)

17.

(*Day.*

The flat is empty. We can hear the sound of shrieking from off.

DANIEL *runs into the living room holding a piece of paper.*

NADIA *enters in hot pursuit.*)

NADIA   Give it back!

(*She goes up to him and tries to snatch the paper. He holds it above his head and stands on tip toes, so it is out of her reach.*)

Child.

DANIEL   You know the rules.

NADIA   Give it back!

DANIEL   A kiss? You sign off a work email with a kiss?

NADIA   Are you jealous?

DANIEL   Yes.

(NADIA *grabs him by his cock.*)

Is that meant to be unpleasant?

(*She squeezes.*)

Okay, now it's starting to hurt.

(*Harder.*)

NADIA   Give. It. Back.

          (*Harder.* DANIEL *winces.*)

DANIEL   No. No work on Mondays.

          (*He places a hand on her groin, keeping the paper
          above his head with the other.*)

NADIA   That's kind of kinky.

DANIEL   Good, kinky? Or bad, kinky?

NADIA   There is no bad kinky.

DANIEL   You still aren't getting it back.

          (*She pushes herself up against him. Puts her mouth
          to his ear. Whispers something.*

          We see DANIEL *smile. In the moment of his
          distraction* NADIA *lets go of his groin, jumps up and
          grabs the paper from him.*)

          You cheat!!

          (NADIA *falls onto the bed with the piece of paper in
          her hands.*)

NADIA   You want it, come and get it.

          (DANIEL *starts to move to the bed provocatively. As
          soon as he is in range* NADIA *drops the paper, grabs
          a pillow and smashes him in the face with it.*)

          Loser!

          (DANIEL *grabs a pillow.*)

DANIEL   Right, that's it.

          (DANIEL *takes a swing with his pillow at* NADIA.
          Misses.

          She gets him again.

          They are both laughing.

          *He swings again and catches her square in the face.
          Hard.*)

Oh fuck, are you okay?

(*She goes down onto the bed, a hand to her eye.*)

Nadia…

(*As he leans down towards her, she takes a huge swing with the pillow and smashes him in the face again. She almost can't breathe with how much she is laughing now.*)

Unbelievable.

(DANIEL *jumps onto the bed and grabs* NADIA *into an embrace. Kisses her.*

A moment.)

NADIA   It was nothing. The email. You don't have to be jealous.

18.

(*Night.*

DANIEL *lies in bed watching TV alone.*

He places his hand under the covers.

Starts to masturbate.)

19.

(*Day.*

The TV is on in the background. It plays loudly. DANIEL *lies on the bed.*

The door opens and NADIA *enters, she dispenses with her coat and shoes in one fluid movement as she speaks.*)

NADIA   We ran late. I'm sorry. I did try to get away.

(*She moves over to* DANIEL *and kisses him, on the cheek.*)

You look comfortable.

DANIEL   I am.

NADIA   Not too comfortable. I want you alert.

DANIEL   Oh, yeah?

(*He sits up in bed, reaches for her.*)

NADIA   But first, I need to pee.

(*He pulls her towards him. Kisses her.*)

Daniel.

DANIEL   What?

NADIA   The toilet. My bladder.

DANIEL   Be quick.

(*She moves off to the toilet. The conversation continues with* NADIA *offstage.*)

NADIA   I'm sorry I couldn't make last week.

DANIEL   It's fine.

NADIA   I did want to see you.

DANIEL   It's fine. Really.

(*Beat.*)

I've actually been quite busy. I know you take the piss, but things are going really well with work at the moment. Me and Steve are thinking about taking someone on.

(NADIA *is stood at the door.*)

Steve. I can barely look at him and keep a straight face.

NADIA   This.

(DANIEL *turns to see her. She holds a child's glove in her hand.*)

What's this?

DANIEL   Where did you find that?

(*He stands and moves towards her. She moves to the other side of the room.*)

It's actually a really funny story.

NADIA   Is it?

(*He moves towards her again, reaches for it. She pulls it away.*)

DANIEL   Can I have it back please?

NADIA   Tell me what it's doing here.

DANIEL   You don't need to be all –

NADIA   What? I don't need to be all what?

DANIEL   I was just in the area. With Danny.

NADIA   *Danny.*

DANIEL   He wasn't feeling well. And I had a key, so I –

NADIA   You brought him here?

DANIEL   We were virtually outside.

NADIA   So you brought him here?

DANIEL   I have a key.

(*She throws the mitten at him.*)

Why is this such a big deal?

NADIA   How can you... Why were you here?

DANIEL   I wasn't. We were just passing and –

NADIA   Has he been here before? Your son.

DANIEL   No.

NADIA   Did *she* bring him here? To meet you?

DANIEL   No!

(*A moment.*)

NADIA   Does she know?

DANIEL   What?

NADIA   It's a very simple fucking question.

(*A silence.*)

Okay. Okay. Does she know it's me?

(*Pause.*)

Does. She. Know. It's me?

DANIEL   No.

NADIA   You're sure?

DANIEL   Yes.

NADIA   Nothing. Not even a hint?

(*Pause.*)

This is my life. My actual life.

DANIEL   Then what the fuck is this? What am I?

NADIA   This is this. And you are you.

DANIEL   What does that mean?

NADIA   Exactly what I just said.

DANIEL   We've been doing *this* for over three years.

NADIA   I know.

(*Beat.*)

And it's not working any more.

DANIEL Don't say that.

NADIA   You brought your fucking child here. Here?!

DANIEL I know. I know that. And I'm sorry.

NADIA   It was never meant to be like this.

DANIEL I said I'm sorry.

(*Pause.*)

NADIA   You've ruined it now.

DANIEL Nadia, can you please just give me a minute to –

NADIA   You need to go.

(*Pause.*)

DANIEL What?

NADIA   Go.

DANIEL I... I don't understand...

NADIA   Leave. Vacate the building. Fuck off. Do you understand now? We're done here.

DANIEL What are you... I love you.

NADIA   You brought him here. You brought him into my life.

DANIEL He's my son.

NADIA   Exactly. And for three years we have managed to keep that –

DANIEL Three years! All that time. Time I was here with you. Away from him. I only did that because I thought this was... And now you just... I never even looked at another woman before you came along. This isn't nothing to me. This isn't just some fling. You aren't just a –

NADIA   There were others.

(*Pause.*)

Before. You. This.

(*A silence.*)

DANIEL   You're lying.

(*She is.*)

NADIA   I'm not saying they meant the same as you. I'm not
saying it was like this. But there have been others.
And when it's done it's done. That's how it has to be.

DANIEL   But you said –

NADIA   And maybe at that exact time I meant it. Everything.
But I have a life, Daniel. With beautiful children.
And a wonderful husband. And I'm not going to give
that away for this.

(*Beat.*)

You knew what this was. We both did.

DANIEL   You make it sound so small.

NADIA   It is. In comparison. You understand. Deep down
you do.

(*Pause.*)

Go back to her. Make it right.

DANIEL   I can't.

NADIA   You can.

DANIEL   I told her I don't love her any more.

NADIA   Tell her you changed your mind.

DANIEL   PEOPLE DON'T JUST CHANGE THEIR MIND
ABOUT THINGS LIKE THAT.

NADIA   Of course they do.

(*Pause.*)

This is when you leave.

DANIEL   You did this before?

(DANIEL *stands for a second. Lost.*)

You heartless fucking cunt.

(*He shakes his head and walks towards the door,
slamming it as he exits.*)

20.

(The flat is empty.

A long pause.

Then the sound of a key in the door can be heard. NADIA *stumbles into the flat. She's obviously been drinking.*

She takes out her phone. Dials a number.

We hear a phone ring.

She follows the noise. It's coming from the bed. She moves the bedsheets and finds DANIEL*'s burner phone there. His key next to it.*

She sits down on the bed.

Gradually the light starts to fade. Night has come.

Followed by morning.

The TV is gone.

Night.

Then the throws.

Day.

The bloodstains on the floor are gone.

Night.

Day.

The curtains are pulled back.

Night.

Day.

Night.

Day.

Night.

Day.

The changing of light is now almost continuous, a blur.

The light starts to build until the flat is blinded from view. As it dims we see the flat is now back to exactly how it was before they moved in. A bare, personality-less flat. The same as any other buy-to-let studio in London. The only relic of them: the small table. Two sets of keys are on it and the pocket watch DANIEL *gave her as an anniversary present.*

NADIA *stands and starts to walk to the door. She places her hand on it. Stops. Turns sharply and makes a dash for the table. Jumps up and stands on it. Laughs to herself. Bittersweet.*

Her phone starts to ring. A moment of hope. Maybe... Just maybe...

She sees the fascia. And it's gone.)

NADIA   Hey...

          (*Pause.*)

          No, I'm nearly finished. I won't be late.

          (*Pause.*)

          Takeaway? That would be lovely.

          (*Pause.*)

          Chinese...

          (*She's crying. She puts her hand to her mouth to cover it.*

          Takes a breath. Composes herself.)

          Nothing. I'll be home soon.

          (*A silence.*)

          I love you too.

          (*Blackout.*)

A Nick Hern Book

Rust first published in Great Britain in 2019 as a paperback original by
Nick Hern Books Limited, The Glasshouse, 49a Goldhawk Road, London
W12 8QP, in association with HighTide Theatre and the Bush Theatre, London

Rust copyright © 2019 Kenny Emson

Kenny Emson has asserted his right to be identified as the author of this work

Cover photography by Claire Pepper
Cover design by Studio Doug

Designed and typeset by Nick Hern Books, London
Printed in Great Britain by Mimeo Ltd, Huntingdon, Cambridgeshire PE29 6XX

A CIP catalogue record for this book is available from the British Library

ISBN 978 1 84842 861 4

Woodland
CARBON
www.woodlandcarbon.co.uk
NICK HERN BOOKS
Printed on Carbon Captured paper